And There Shall Be Signs...

Treasures of The Vatican Library
(Book Illustration, Volume 8)

And There Shall Be Signs. . .

Turner Publishing, Inc.

ATLANTA

The illustrations in this book are taken from the Latin manuscript volumes in the collections
of The Vatican Library, including the Barberini, Chigi, Reginense, and Urbino collections.
The sources for each illustration appear on page 80.

Published by Turner Publishing, Inc.
A Subsidiary of Turner Broadcasting System, Inc.
1050 Techwood Drive, N.W.
Atlanta, Georgia 30318

First Edition 10 9 8 7 6 5 4 3 2 1

Library of Congress Cataloging-in-Publication Data
And there shall be signs . . .
p. cm.—(Treasures of the Vatican Library)
Contains illustrations from various Vatican Library manuscripts with each illustration
accompanied by a Bible scripture from the New Revised Standard Version Bible.
ISBN 1-57036-234-3 (alk. paper).
1. Astrology in art.   2. Zodiac in art.   3. Illumination of books and
manuscripts, Medieval.   4. Illumination of books and
manuscripts—Vatican City.   5. Biblioteca apostolica vaticana.
I. Biblioteca apostolica vaticana.   II. Turner Publishing, Inc.
III. Bible. English. New Revised Standard. Selections. 1995.   IV. Series.
ND3333.A53   1995
745.6'7'0940902—dc20   95-220
CIP

Printed in the Hong Kong.

Treasures of The Vatican Library:
Book Illustration

$\mathcal{A}$ND THERE SHALL BE SIGNS..., the eighth volume in the Treasures of The Vatican Library series, offers a selection of miniature masterworks of book illustration from the collections of one of the world's greatest repositories of classical, medieval, and Renaissance culture. The Vatican Library, for six hundred years celebrated as a center of learning and a monument to the art of the book, is, nevertheless, little known to the general public, for admission to the library traditionally has been restricted to qualified scholars. Since very few outside the scholarly community have ever been privileged to examine the magnificent hand-lettered and illuminated manuscript books in the library's collections, the artwork selected for the series volumes is all the more poignant, fascinating, and appealing.

Of course, the popes had always maintained a library, but in the fifteenth century, Pope Nicholas V decided to build an edifice of unrivaled magnificence to house the papacy's growing collections—to serve the entire "court of Rome," the clerics and scholars associated with the papal palace. Pope Sixtus IV added to what Nicholas had begun, providing the library with a suite of beautifully frescoed rooms and furnishing it with heavy wooden benches, to which the precious works were actually chained. But, most significantly, like the popes who succeeded him, Sixtus added books. By 1455 the library held 1,200 volumes, and a catalogue compiled in 1481 listed 3,500, making it by far the largest collection of books in the Western world.

And The Vatican Library has kept growing: through purchase, commission, donation, and military conquest. Nor did the popes restrict themselves to ecclesiastical subjects. Bibles, theological texts, and commentaries on canon law are here in abundance, to be sure, but so are the Latin and Greek classics that placed The Vatican Library at the very heart of all Renaissance learning. Over the centuries, the library has acquired some of the world's most significant collections of literary works, including the Palatine Library of Heidelberg, the Cerulli collection of Persian and Ethiopian manuscripts, the great Renaissance libraries of the Duke of Urbino and of Queen Christiana of Sweden, and the matchless seventeenth-century collections of the Barberini, the Ottoboni, and Chigi. Today the library contains over one million printed books — including eight thousand published during the first fifty years of the printing press — in addition to 150,000 manuscripts and some 100,000 prints. Assiduously collected and carefully preserved over the course of almost six hundred years, these unique works of art and knowledge, ranging from the secular to the profane, are featured in this ongoing series, Treasures of The Vatican Library, for the delectation of lovers of great books and breathtaking works of art.

*A great portent
appeared in heaven:
a woman clothed with
the sun, with the moon
under her feet, and on
her head a crown of
twelve stars.*

—REVELATION 12:1

And when you
look up to the heavens
and see the sun, the moon,
and the stars, all the host
of heaven, do not be led
astray and bow down to
them and serve them, things
that the Lord your God has
allotted to all the peoples
everywhere under heaven.

—DEUTERONOMY 4:19

"There will be signs in the sun, the moon, and the stars.... People will faint from fear and foreboding of what is coming upon the world, for the powers of the heavens will be shaken."

—LUKE 21:25–26

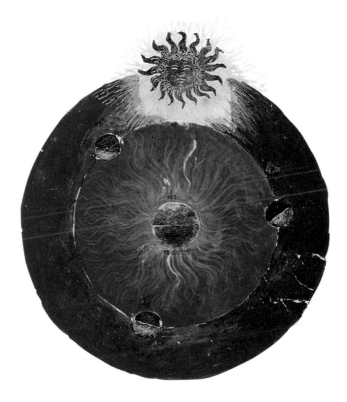

... to know the structure of the world and the activity of the elements; the beginning and end and middle of times, the alternations of the solstices and the changes of the seasons, the cycles of the year and the constellations of the stars....

—THE WISDOM OF SOLOMON 7:17–19

You are wearied
with your many
consultations; let those
who study the heavens
stand up and save you,
those who gaze at the
stars, and at each new
moon predict what
shall befall you.

—ISAIAH 47:13

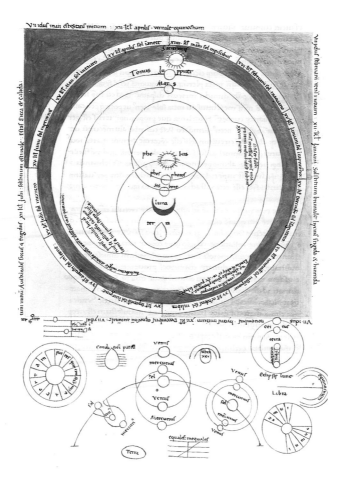

Incipiunt figure eclypsium solis

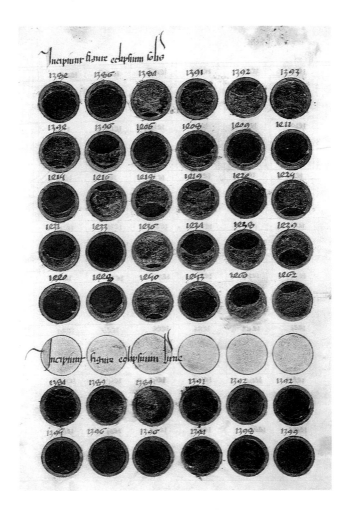

Incipiunt figure eclypsium lune

The new moon, as its name suggests, renews itself; how marvelous it is in this change, a beacon to the hosts on high, shining in the vault of the heavens!

—SIRACH 43:8

There are both heavenly
bodies and earthly bodies,
but the glory of the heavenly
is one thing, and that of the
earthly is another. There is
one glory of the sun, and
another glory of the moon,
and another glory of the
stars; indeed, star differs
from star in glory.

—1 CORINTHIANS 15:40-41

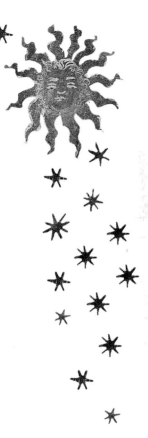

The glory of the stars
is the beauty of heaven,
a glittering array in
the heights of the Lord.
On the orders of the
Holy One they stand in
their appointed places;
they never relax in
their watches.

—SIRACH 43:9-10

And God said, "Let there
be lights in the dome of
the sky to separate the
day from the night; and
let them be for signs and
for seasons and for days
and years, and let them
be lights in the dome of
the sky to give light
upon the earth."

—GENESIS 1:14-15

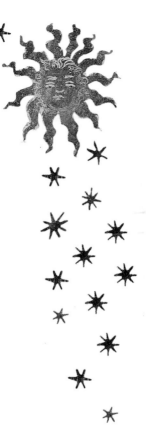

For everything
there is a season, and
a time for every matter
under heaven: a time to
be born, and a time to
die; a time to plant, and
a time to pluck up what
is planted.

—ECCLESIASTES 3:1–2

ARIES

MARCH 21—APRIL 20

For before the harvest,

when the blossom is over

and the flower becomes

a ripening grape, he will

cut off the shoots with

pruning hooks, and the

spreading branches he

will hew away.

—ISAIAH 18:5

Mars ha .xxi. iour
La lune .xxx.

m	d		Saint aubin
xi	e	n	
	g	fii	
xix	g	iii	
viii	a b	ii	
xvi	d	id	
v	c	id	
	f	id	
xiii	g	id	
ii	a	id	Saint gregoire
x	b	id	
	c	id	
xviii	d	id	
vii	e	kl	
	f	kl	
xv	g	kl	
iiii	a	kl	
	b	kl	Saint benoit.
xii	d	kl	
i	e	kl	
	f	kl	
ix	g	kl	Lamutation nře dae
	a	kl	
xvii	b	kl	Saint legier
vi	c	kl	
	d	kl	
xiiii	e	kl	
iii	f	kl	

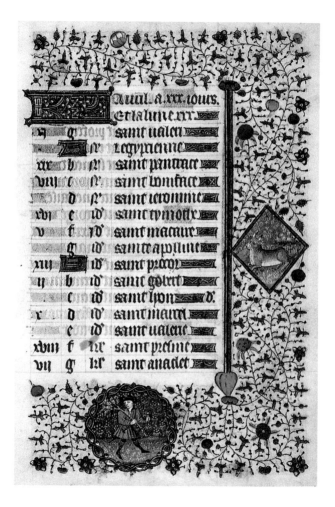

KL Auril a .xxx. iours.
et la lune .xxx.

a			saint valeri
			le grip riaine
xix	b		saint pancrace
viij	c		saint boniface
	d		saint ieronime
xvi	e	id'	saint tymothe
v	f	id'	saint macaire
	g	id'	saint apolline
xiij		id'	saint pzeor
ij	b	id'	saint gobert
	c	id'	saint lyon
x	d	id'	saint maurel
	e	id'	saint valere
xviij	f	ke	saint presine
vij	g	ke	saint anaclet

TAURUS

APRIL 21—MAY 21

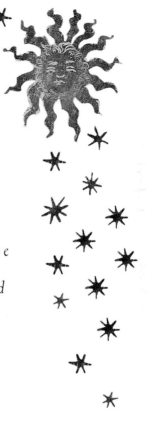

Let us go out early to
the vineyards, and see
whether the vines have
budded, whether the grape
blossoms have opened and
the pomegranates are in
bloom. There I will give
you my love.

—SONG OF SOLOMON 7:12

GEMINI

MAY 22—JUNE 21

Do not abandon old friends, for new ones cannot equal them. A new friend is like new wine; when it has aged, you can drink it with pleasure.

—SIRACH 9:10

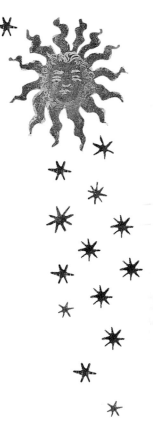

CANCER
June 22—July 23

"But when the grain is ripe, at once he goes in with his sickle, because the harvest has come."

—Mark 4:29

LEO

JULY 24—AUGUST 23

The point is this: the one who sows sparingly will also reap sparingly, and the one who sows bountifully will also reap bountifully.

—2 CORINTHIANS 9:6

VIRGO

AUGUST 24—SEPTEMBER 23

"You shall come to your
grave in ripe old age,
as a shock of grain comes
up to the threshing floor
in its season."

—JOB 5:26

LIBRA

SEPTEMBER 24—OCTOBER 23

As you lock up

your silver and gold,

so make balances and

scales for your words.

—SIRACH 28:24B–25A

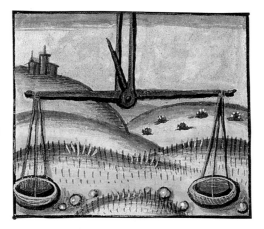

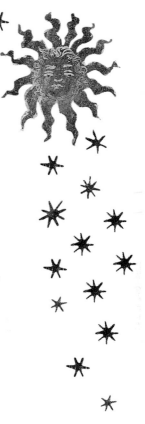

SCORPIO

OCTOBER 24—NOVEMBER 22

In the morning sow your
seed, and at evening
do not let your hands be
idle; for you do not know
which will prosper, this
or that, or whether both
alike will be good.

—ECCLESIASTES 11:6

SAGITTARIUS

NOVEMBER 23 — DECEMBER 21

Can one turn back

an arrow shot by a

strong archer?

—2 ESDRAS 16:7

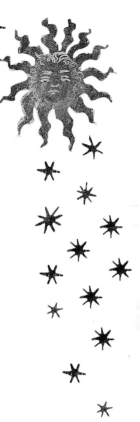

CAPRICORN

DECEMBER 22—JANUARY 20

You see me and test me—

my heart is with you.

Pull them out like sheep

for the slaughter, and set

them apart for the day

of slaughter.

—JEREMIAH 12:3

Aquarius

JANUARY 21—FEBRUARY 19

Your threshing shall

overtake the vintage,

and the vintage shall

overtake the sowing;

you shall eat your bread

to the full, and live

securely in your land.

—LEVITICUS 26:5

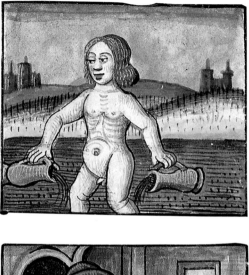

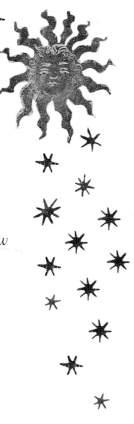

PISCES

FEBRUARY 20 — MARCH 20

"As I have seen, those
who plow iniquity and sow
trouble reap the same."

—JOB 4:8

The one who made
the Pleiades and Orion,
and turns deep darkness
into the morning, and
darkens the day into
night, who calls for the
waters of the sea, and
pours them out on the
surface of the earth, the
Lord is his name.

—AMOS 5:8

He said, "Let
the earth be made,"
and it was made,
and "Let the heaven be
made," and it was made.
At his word the stars
were fixed in their places,
and he knows the number
of the stars.

—2 ESDRAS 16:55–56

From the moon comes
the sign for festal days,
a light that wanes when
it completes its course.

—SIRACH 43:7

"For false messiahs
and false prophets will
appear and produce great
signs and omens, to lead
astray, if possible,
even the elect."

—Matthew 24:24

You have made people
like the fish of the sea,
like crawling things
that have no ruler.

—HABAKKUK 1:14

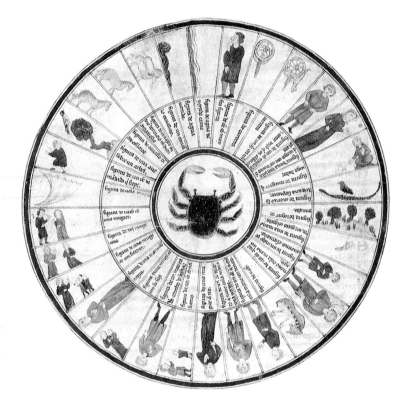

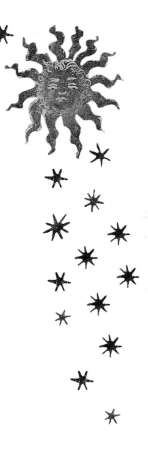

...the whole world
before you is like a
speck that tips the
scales, and like a drop
of morning dew that
falls on the ground.

—THE WISDOM OF SOLOMON 11:22

For God loves nothing
so much as the person
who lives with wisdom.
She is more beautiful
than the sun, and excels
every constellation
of the stars.

—THE WISDOM OF SOLOMON 7:28–29

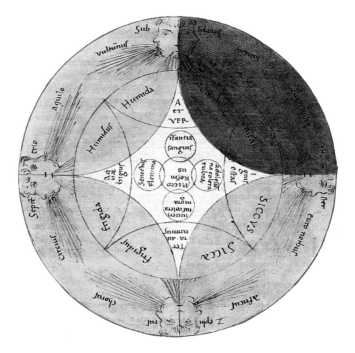

For sun and moon
and stars are bright,
and when sent to do a
service, they are obedient.
So also the lightning,
when it flashes, is widely
seen; and the wind likewise
blows in every land.

—THE LETTER OF JEREMIAH 1:60–61

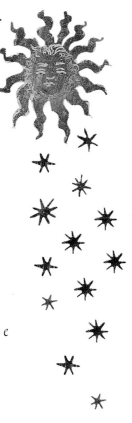

Since you know then
that they are not gods,
do not fear them. They
can neither curse nor
bless kings; they cannot
show signs in the heavens
for the nations, or shine
like the sun or give light
like the moon.

—THE LETTER OF JEREMIAH 1:65–67

The moon in heaven,

with the stars, does not

stand so august as you,

who, after lighting the way

of your starlike seven sons

to piety, stand in honor

before God and are firmly

set in heaven with them.

—4 Maccabees 17:5

You have made the
moon to mark the
seasons; the sun knows
its time for setting.

—PSALM 104:19

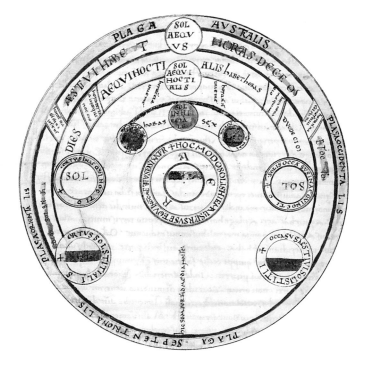

OHMO Maestro creator verace
per chui & cielo & terra facti sono
& cioche messa sicontiene & tace
concedi pertua gratia & pertuo dono
cheio possa seguittare come ate piace
conchiato stile & con apecto suono
afigurare laterra elmare euenti
siche senabbia buoni intendimenti
Fannosi quatro plaghe permostrare
tisti della terra & ogni parte
dellotriente uerso elcoricare
sifanno cinque cone malcuna arte
& otto uenti sono pernauigare
monti principali & meçi & parte
questi nessanno lume aben uedere
daqual parte lacosa deicomprendere
Ceffiro e quello che noi chiaman potente
& choro maestrale & aquilone
tramontana sichiama & seghuente
borbea desto greco euro sipone
pre loleuante & noto incontanente
sisloche a nome & seguitta africone
che cimeçcocch elultimo e del chiostro
lebrecto ouee cheebmo che sidice ostro

plaga settentrionale

plaga orientale

plaga occidentale

plaga meridionale

greco leuante

noto scilocco

tramontana aquilone

ostro meço di

effiro ponente

choro maestrale

lubecco africo

The heavens are
telling the glory of
God; and the firmament
proclaims his handiwork.
Day to day pours forth
speech, and night to night
declares knowledge.

—Psalm 19:1–2

I will show portents in

the heavens and on the

earth, blood and fire

and columns of smoke.

The sun shall be turned

to darkness, and the

moon to blood, before

the great and terrible

day of the Lord comes.

—JOEL 2:30–31

magnitudie ⁊ uirtute tc̄ suā collom
uit q̄ liᵉt stellis ut par̄ l̄i ī figa.

Sexto decl̄ar id̄ ī siḡ chūo q̄d e
leo dicō leo h̄eculeꝰ ⁊ s̄m h̄au
les nāscit aᵭ deꝰ flāmigꝰ est
hꝰ. q̄ sole exsystem̄ ī leone. ⁊ max
im̄ cālor. tūc ⁊ sequit̄ dies cāni
culares. ⁊ cū cadet de celo. de c̄o
leone suph̄iꝰ ē. ⁊ tḡ ·i· cōt· vij·
q̄uto de ·vj· signo aᵭ ē ꝟ̄go dia
cadet ꝟ̄go. ⁊ blāce astrea fiha
ob estatē mūcādā ⁊ trāś ī lic̄
teꝭ. h̄ dic̄ q̄a ultia ecc̄te de m̄.
duū pecc̄ h̄eam diꝰ p̄ mīa
malicie habūdātia. ⁊ ꝟ̄go trā
deꝰ ut · vij· diē cū s̄. de custodia
ultiā celestū ⁊ erat astrea relig
chūo de sept̄o signo aᵭ c̄ lus̄ ⁊
dic̄ dicō ⁊ p̄oiā īste libᵃ eadē
libᵃ ⁊ sept̄ī siḡ ē coū. h̄ ꝟ̄go
astᵃ · mᵃ hō · ꝓdanē ⁊ souū p̄e
sentas̄ · h̄ duo signa luceū ut p̄ ī
sulnecta figa.

Septio de siḡ · ix· aᵭ c̄ sagittariᵘ
subdit̄ ⁊ chūo seneꝰ chūo tuū cō
uenit̄ ⁊ educetꝰ achilles aᵭ teū ꝑ
uaū speculas̄ · ⁊ pēnatas sagitta
neruo h̄emonio · ⁊ thessaliā ab
hemo mōte dc̄o h̄emomo ꝑder spi
cula ⁊ uipto nūo h̄eules hospitaū
⁊pᵭ chūone p̄natur s̄m sagittā
toxicatas leruco spēe q̄d dū cō
trectꝟ chūo iuua sᵘpede ē tetā
dit · eiꝰ dolore ulᷓme niū uga
ree · ⁊ mori n̄ post ūflacone doū
ⁱūstᷓe aᵭ sibi fulgē stell̄ · xlj · ut
ī sulnecta descꝰone.

Octauo de signo · x· ⁊ · xj· subdic̄ ge
lidus egelocus · i· capricornū ege
reus · ⁊ reducens · h̄iemē p̄gm̄
⁊ q̄ p̄is̄ facit cadet h̄augetā
tuū uꝰuā cuius̄ms es · s· q̄eam

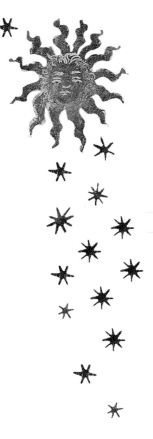

"*So do not worry about tomorrow, for tomorrow will bring worries of its own. Today's trouble is enough for today.*"

—MATTHEW 6:34

ILLUSTRATIONS

Cover and frontispiece: Barb. Lat. 76 fol. 3 r; p. 7: Urb. Lat. 752 fol. 4 v; p. 9: Urb. Lat. 329 fol. 131 v; p. 10: Urb. Lat. 752 fol. 3 v; p. 13: Urb. Lat. 752 fol. 7 r; p. 14: Vat. Lat. 681 fol. 96 r; p. 17: Urb. Lat. 329 fol. 139 v; p. 18: Reg. Lat. 155 fol. 17 r; p. 21: Urb. Lat. 1358 fol. 3 r; p. 22: Urb. Lat. 752 fol. 4 v; p. 25: Urb. Lat. 752 fol. 11 v; p. 26: Vat. Lat. 643 fol. 98 r; p. 29: Barb. Lat. 487 fol. 2 r; p. 30: Chigi C IV 109 fol. 4 r; p. 33: Barb. Lat. 487 fol. 3 r; p. 34: Chigi C IV 109 fol. 6 r; p. 37: Barb. Lat. 487 fol. 4 r; p. 38: Chigi C IV 109 fol. 8 r; p. 41: Barb. Lat. 487 fol. 5 r; p. 42: Chigi C IV 109 fol. 10 r; p. 45: Barb. Lat. 487 fol. 6 r; p. 46: Chigi C IV 109 fol. 12 r; p. 49: Barb. Lat. 487 fol. 1 r; p. 50: Chigi C IV 109 fol. 2 r; p. 53: Barb. Lat. 76 fol. 29 r; p. 54: Reg. Lat. 438 fol. 34 v; p. 57: Urb. Lat. 752 fol. 7 v; p. 58: Barb. Lat. 76 fol. 14 v; p. 61: Reg. Lat. 1283 fol. 3 v; p. 62: Reg. Lat. 1283 fol. 6 v; p. 65: Barb. Lat. 76 fol. 31 r; p. 66: Urb. Lat. 329 fol. 133 r; p. 69: Barb. Lat. 76 fol. 21 r; p. 70: Vat. Lat. 1650 fol. 58 r; p. 73: Reg. Lat. 123 fol. 162 v; p. 74: Urb. Lat. 752 fol. 15 r; p. 77: Urb. Lat. 752 fol. 9 v; p. 78: Vat. Lat. 1650 fol. 57 r. Ornamental illumination on pp. 8, 12, 16, 20, 24, 28, 32, 36, 40, 44, 48, 52, 56, 60, 64, 68, 72, and 76 is from Barb. Lat. 487 fol. 1 r. Ornamental illumination on pp. 11, 15, 19, 23, 27, 31, 35, 39, 43, 47, 51, 55, 59, 63, 67, 71, 75, and 79 is from Urb. Lat. 752 fol. 3 v.